Cornish Guernseys & Knit-frocks

Mary Wright

Alison Hodge in association with Ethnographica Ltd.

First published in 1979, in hardback by Ethnographica, 19 Westbourne
Road, London N7 8AN, and in paperback by Alison Hodge, Bosulval,
Newmill, Penzance, Cornwall TR20 8XA.
First published 1979. Reprinted 1980, 1981, 1983, 1986, 1988.

ISBN 0-906720 05 2 (paperback); 0-905788 07 9 (hardback).
Origination by Ethnographica Ltd. Designer: Stuart Hamilton.
Printed and bound by A. Wheaton & Co. Ltd, Exeter.

ACKNOWLEDGEMENTS

I acknowledge with thanks the help of all who have searched their
memories and their attics on my behalf, especially Joan Hart of
the Lizard, Kay Jolliff and Sheila de Burlet of Polperro, Mollie
Goodway of Sennen, Mabel Jenkins of Liskeard and Charles
Nicholas of Looe.

I was accorded research facilities by Richard Poppleton and
Sons Ltd., Wakefield, Yorkshire; the County Records Office,
Truro; Cornwall Local History Library, Redruth (Mr. T. Knight);
the Royal Institution of Cornwall (Mr. H.L. Douch), and
Launceston Library, whose staff were particularly helpful. The
Cornish Times Newspapers, Liskeard, the West Briton
Newspapers, Truro, and the Packet Newspapers, Falmouth, also
gave me access to their records.

For permission to use photographs, I am indebted to Messrs.
T. Hart, C. Daniels, M. Trenerry, A.E. Raddy; Mesdames
D. Heard, A. Harris, R. Scott, F. Cowan, N. Blake, J. Buckley,
D. Tearney and K. Jolliff; the Rowett Institute, Polperro; the
Royal Institution of Cornwall (especially H.L. Douch and
R. Penhallurick); the Royal National Lifeboat Institution, and
Bude Historical and Folk Exhibition. The Sutcliffe Gallery,
Whitby, North Yorkshire gave me permission to reproduce the
photograph of Henry Freeman on p. 56.

I am particularly grateful to Andrew Lanyon for careful
reproduction of old photographs and endless patience in
photographing my knitting stitches.

For the loan of knitting sticks, I thank Messrs. George Hawken,
Charles Nicholas, Harding and Coad; Miss K. Spear; Mesdames
Tremain, Sleep, Trathen, Hoskins, Bartlett, Edmunds, Gerry and
Oliver.

The continued interest of members of the Cornwall Federation
of Women's Institutes is sincerely appreciated.

Finally, my thanks are offered to Alison Hodge for her typing
and advice in preparation of the manuscript.

Contents

Symbols

These symbols are used in the charts which accompany the knitting instructions given in this book.

☐   knit

⊠   purl

—   cable

⊟   slip 1 knitwise

▨   slip 1 purlwise

⊞   knit 1 into row below

▩   purl 1 into row below

Abbreviations

The following abbreviations are used in the knitting instructions for the Cornish patterns (pp.31-54), the basic guernsey pattern (**pp.63-5**) and the Polperro knit frock (pp.66-7).

K. = knit; P. = purl;

st. (s) = stitch (es)

st.-st. = stocking stitch (all rounds knit in circular knitting; knit 1 row, purl 1 row in 2-way knitting);

inc. = increase by lifting the strand between 2 stitches on to left-hand needle and knitting into the back of it with the right-hand needle;

dec. = decrease by working 2 stitches together.

L.H. = left hand; R.H. = right hand;

O.R.L. = or required length;

sl. = slip;

moss = K.1, P.1 on alternate sts. on alternate rows;

K.1B = knit 1 below (knit into loop below stitch on needle and lift off both loops together); P.1B = purl 1 below (purl into loop below stitch on needle and lift off both loops together);

K.8F = cable 8 by slipping 4 sts. on to cable needle and leaving at front of work, K.4 sts. from L.H. needle, K.4 sts. from cable needle.

cm = centimetre (s);   in (s) = inch (es);   cont. = continue.

The 1872 photograph of a Lizard fisherman from which I was asked to copy a guernsey.

Introduction

I did not intend to write a book; I simply wanted to knit a guernsey similar to those knitted by Cornish women over a hundred years ago. In the past, hand-knitting was vital to the domestic economy of every Cornish fishing family, and patterns and techniques were handed down from mother to daughters. Girls began to knit at an early age and there was no need for written instructions. But times have changed and we no longer remember all the old skills.

In the last fifty years or so, Cornwall has become more affluent and her women have found more lucrative employment than knitting. Although hand-knitted guernseys are still among the most hard-wearing of garments, mass-produced clothes are readily available, offering more choice, if not at a saving in cost, certainly at a saving in time and labour.

Although partly to blame for the decline of traditional techniques, the introduction of domestic knitting machines with their speed and seeming infinite formulae for patterns in punch cards and colour changes, and of 'quick knits' with large needles and thick yarns, reflect the adaptability of the craft and have no doubt contributed to its continuing popularity. Today, hand-knitting is one of the most widely-practised crafts in this country. It is not only a means of making garments, but a therapeutic exercise with its repetitive, conventional technique, and a stimulating art form with its wide variety of textures and coloured yarns.

In recent years there has been a considerable move away from the continual wearing of mass-produced clothes, and an increasing appreciation of 'ethnic' fashions, accompanied by a growing interest in relearning old hand crafts. Gossamer lace knitting from the Shetland Islands, superb colour patterns from Fair Isle and the bold textured surfaces of Aran knitting prove that traditional knitting patterns and techniques have never been quite lost, and it was amid this revival of interest in past skills that I undertook to knit a Cornish guernsey.

In 1970, I was asked to copy a knitted fisherman's guernsey from an old photograph, as a contribution to a Women's Institute display at the Royal Cornwall Show. I was unfamiliar with this specialised form of knitting, and at that time it seemed impossible to find anyone in Cornwall who remembered the knitting or the knitters. Mr. Charles Nicholas of Looe warned me that I had started twenty years too late.

Gladys Thompson's book, *Patterns for Guernseys and Jerseys*, gave extensive information about patterns from the north and north-east of England which she had researched more than thirty years ago. Her charts, pictures and anecdotes revealed a fascinating insight into the knitters of that area over the last one hundred years. Pattern leaflets from the Channel Islands gave more specific details of the yarn used and tensions required and, after many experiments, I was able to combine this information with wool purchased from Guernsey (manufactured in Yorkshire) and pattern stitches from the photograph to produce my first Cornish guernsey. This was completed during winter evenings with the 'aid' of modern artificial light, but I have since learned that the best results are achieved by knitting out of doors, in day light, as traditional knitters used to do.

'Tomorrow's Heirlooms', a national Women's Institute exhibition in 1975, provided the next challenge, with a section devoted to research in a traditional craft. With increasing public interest in the first guernsey, additional information slowly drifting in and more photographs being discovered, I was convinced that there was sufficient scope for a serious study of guernsey knitting in Cornwall. This county, which spans nearly one hundred miles from the Tamar to Land's End, and has a

My first Cornish guernsey, copied from the Lizard pattern in 1972 and worn by Mr. R. Renouf.

2

coastline of over two hundred and seventy miles, provides a natural stimulus for any research project related to the sea and seafarers.

Guernseys are not exclusive to Cornwall. In fact, their use and wear throughout the British Isles for at least a century and a half almost justifies qualification for a national costume. However, by concentrating on this one local region, I have discovered and recorded more than twenty-four principal patterns, and some fascinating background information about Cornish knitting and knitters since the beginning of the nineteenth century.

The patterns have been recorded according to the *place* in which they were first found. Duplications are inevitable within the county, and the same designs have been noted at Bude and Sennen Cove, Polperro and the Lizard, Boscastle and Porthgwarra. No doubt some of the designs resemble those found in other parts of the country, and I attribute this to two reasons: (a) fishermen travelled to and from Cornwall throughout their working lives, especially to ports in the north-east; a few settled 'away' and a few brought wives from 'away';* and (b) it is quite probable that a knitter from Cornwall, working in isolation, would produce designs similar to those of another knitter because all patterns are combinations of simple plain and purl stitches, and ropes, chains, waves, nets and sand-prints would provide visual inspiration.

Memories have proved surprisingly vivid, especially those of older men in the fishing villages. They were able to remember their boyhood and their grandmothers with particular clarity and must have watched and listened through many knitting hours. They remembered the knitting of pockets for men's watches – 'they work better when they're warm'; and the 'vamping' of stockings, where the worn heel and foot were removed and a new section knitted on from the old leg. These men could often name each one of a group of fishermen in a photograph taken at the turn of the century. Names were frequently duplicated in a small community and nearly all had nicknames. Five Charles Jolliffs in Polperro at one time were known as Dyer, Geary, Fay, Cubert and Charles.

One of the greatest rewards in a research project of this nature is in meeting people who are genuinely interested in the past and willing to share their memories and experiences. Through Women's Institutes and local history groups, casual acquaintances, and family, friends and relations, I have been fortunate in making many contacts over the past eight years which have culminated in the discovery of an aspect of Cornish life and social history which has not previously been recorded.

Old men in the fishing villages recalled their boyhood...
Jimmy 'Molly' Curtis of Polperro.

---

* Mob-rule was imposed at Newlyn in May 1896 during a violent confrontation between local fishermen and a fleet of Lowestoft boats over Sunday fishing.

Research

A meeting with the late Mr. Jim Honey at Port Isaac in September 1975:

'Excuse me. Do you remember any knitting like this?'
'I should think I do – my Granny knitted hundreds.'
    'Can you tell me anything about them?'
'She only knitted for her own. They were masterpieces and they were all different. She knitted a hole in the front...'
    'What for?'
'For the pocket watches. All her boys had one (jerseys). Uncle Willie lost hi

couldn't find it anywhere and Granny was mad. She had a stall every week at Rock and Padstow markets. Twelve months after, Granny saw a man wearing Uncle Willie's jersey. "Here", she said, "you' got my boy's jersey on." "I hab'n," he said. "Yes, you have," she said, and called a policeman to arrest him. "How do you know this is your boy's jersey?" the policeman asked. "You make'n lift up his arms," said Granny. "You'll see I knitted a 'W' under one arm and an 'S' under the other and my boy's name is Willie Steer – what's his?"

Frocks and Jerseys

> To prosecute his labours, the fisherman must be provided with his outfit: how is this secured? To screen his body from piercing winds, loving fingers are busy knitting a strong, warm worsted frock or jersey, also long, comfortable stockings. But worsted is a poor shelter from the drenching spray and driving rain, so there is a demand on the females for the supply of other garments. A 'jumper' is made of 'duck' and over both is the 'oiler', a covering of 'unbleached' made waterproof. For his head there is a 'sou'wester' of oiled cloth, well padded inside with flannel; while strong 'sea-boots' reaching his thighs, complete his usual costume.
>
> VEALL AND HARRIS, *Porthleven, Past and Present*

Fishermen's knitted garments throughout the British Isles have always been recognisable by their colour and shape. On quays, in harbours and in boats, the navy guernsey is a familiar sight, and is worn not only as a tradition, but for the quality of the knitted fabric. Modern machine-made guernseys and traditional hand-knitted ones have in common both colour and the fine texture of the knitted fabric which resists strong sunshine, salt water, sea air and biting winds.

The shape of the garment is basically square, reminiscent of smocks worn by land workers many years ago. The absence of a curved armhole and inset sleeve results in a dropped shoulder line, sometimes accentuated by a pattern band.

The use of the names 'guernsey' and 'jersey' reflects the strong influence and tradition of the knitting industry of these Channel Islands during the seventeenth, eighteenth and nineteenth centuries. Close trading and shipping links ensured a wide acceptance of the knitting, wearing and naming of the garment. Yet even within the county of Cornwall the name of the garment varies considerably. A

...for his head there is a 'sou'wester' of oiled cloth... Thomas Pender, second coxswain of the Sennen Cove lifeboat and 27 times on active service. Photograph by Preston of Penzance. 1921.

5

'guernsey' or 'gansey' is the most common; a jersey refers to a similar garment knitted in a finer wool or in a different colour.

Peculiar to Polperro is the name 'knit-frock'. It is the only name used by older locals, and in a B.B.C. 'Down Your Way' broadcast in 1973, the conductor of the Polperro Fishermen's Choir mentioned that, 'the boys wear their knit-frocks when they sing, and they get a bit hot sometimes.' From Newlyn, the name 'worsted-frock' was remembered. The word 'frock' was used throughout the nineteenth century to describe a man's knitted garment as opposed to a sewn one. It was often

'Knit-frock' is the only name used by older Polperro men. Thomas 'Doctor' Holten, Joseph 'Dasher' Puckey and Phil Burnett.

acked on to another word for greater emphasis, for example frock-shirt, Guernsey-
rock, Jersey-frock, as illustrated in newspaper reports of that time:

> *October 1865:* FOUND, near New House in the parish of Morval, on
> Wednesday night last, a bundle of clothing, containing two frock-
> shirts, pair trousers, waistcoat, shirt, leggings and leather belt.

> *August 1858, at Cornwall Lammas Assizes*: William Walsh, 20, for
> stealing one cloth coat, one cloth trousers, one cloth waistcoat, one
> Guernsey-frock, two shirts, two prints, one neck-tie and one pocket
> handkerchief, the property of James Carter of Illogan – 2 months'
> hard labour.

> *1860, Cornwall Epiphany Sessions:* fourteen-year old Henry Coles
> was sentenced to one month's hard labour for stealing a guernsey-
> frock, the property of David Hoare, from the smack *Happy Return* at
> Newquay.

In 1862, Michael Cosgrave, aged seventeen, was sentenced to three months' hard
labour 'for stealing a frock' at St. Ives.

The eccentric vicar of Morwenstow in the mid nineteenth century, the Reverend
Robert Stephen Hawker, refused to wear conventional clerical garb and preferred
to wear, under a three-quarter length coat, a 'blue fisherman's jersey' to indicate
that he was 'a fisher of men'. He also chose to wear socks made from wool from his
one black ewe, 'which can supply me with twenty-one pairs of socks every year if I
needed so many.' The wool was spun locally by women at Wellcombe and knitted
'from a pattern sock' by the children of St. Mark's School.

A guernsey, although basically a working garment, was an acceptable and
respectable form of dress for special occasions. At the Fishermen's Chapel in
Porthleven, men wore guernseys to Sunday services within living memory; seamen
wore their best guernseys for family photographs, and a bridal shirt was a special
one made by the bride for her husband. Photographs reveal many interesting
accessories to guernseys, including hand-knitted braces, brocade waistcoats,
cravats, jackets and a wide variety of head-gear from knitted caps to top hats!

The yarn used for making guernseys is dark navy worsted, in four- and five-ply. It
is not, as some people believe, an oiled yarn, but relies on a tight spinning twist and
a closely knitted fabric for its weatherproof qualities.

Richard Poppleton and Sons, Spinners and Dyers of hand knitting wools in
Wakefield, Yorkshire, have been manufacturing this specialised yarn for more than
130 years. In an old ledger dated 24 August, 1846, a worsted yarn listed as '0½' was
quoted at 1s. 9d. per pound (9 pence per 450g). Today, '0½' worsted is still sold in
four- and five-ply for knitters of guernseys, and retails at 75 pence per 50g.

Reverend Robert Stephen Hawker of Morwenstow, aged 60, wearing, under a three-quarter length coat, a 'blue fisherman's jersey' to indicate that he was a 'fisher of men'.

Seamen wore their best knit-frocks for
family photographs. Thomas and
Elizabeth Mark of Polperro with their
children Joan, Nell, Mary, Kate, John and
Tom. Tom became a lay preacher and was
called the 'fishermen's bishop'. The caps
were known as 'cheese cutters'. 1890.

These two boys pose for the photographer in
their knit-frocks. In the knit-frock on the left,
note how the ribbed pattern is continued at
the top of the sleeve.

Schools of Industry

Bradford, Thursday: The commerce of the country has been suffering from strong intermittent fever during this week. Pulse previously irregular, recovered weak steadiness on Monday, patient in fair state on Tuesday morning, recurrence of fever fit, with partial symptoms of paralysis, in the evening, and on Wednesday a state of deplorable prostration....

WOOL MARKET REPORT, *Cornish Times*
February 1865

During the seventeenth century, the people of the Channel Islands had large flocks of sheep and developed a specialised combing and spinning process to produce yarn suitable for knitting. Gradually, the knitters required more yarn than local sources could supply and an Act of Parliament in 1660 determined the quantity which could be imported from England. Consequently, the Islanders relied more and more upon the mainland for supplies of yarn, and concentrated their own efforts on the development of the hand-knitting industry which thrived until the twentieth century.

Towards the end of the seventeenth century, Cornwall established an interest in hand-spinning, using the wool from local sheep, particularly in the north and east of the county. The yarn was offered for public sale and weighing at local weekly markets. Serge-makers, wool merchants and manufacturers from Devon and Cornwall were the principal buyers, and the regular trading outlets made important economic contributions to Liskeard and similar small market towns.

Country people were involved in spinning the wool by hand into yarn. Small groups of women received consignments of raw wool for carding and spinning at home. If necessary, a card or 'turn' (spinning wheel) could be borrowed for one penny a week, which was later deducted from the wages. The spun yarn was taken to a local spinning house at prescribed intervals and exchanged for payment and fresh supplies of raw material. In addition to large numbers of women thus employed in spinning, others were engaged in 'preaching, pricking and crooking' the cards for them. Children were involved in this work, too.

With the introduction of the spinning-jenny and other machinery at the end of the eighteenth century, hand spinners were less in demand and the loss of employment was severely felt. It is from this time that hand-knitting developed as

A 'school of industry' was established for the very poor, and the girls learned knitting.

an alternative source of skill, occupation and income in Cornwall. In 1790, the Fox and Tregelles families of Falmouth established a 'school of industry' for the very poor, mostly girls, 'to learn knitting, etc.' It was maintained by public subscription and accommodated about sixty children at a time.

Dame schools existed to give a rudimentary form of learning to pupils at a fee of twopence (one new penny) a week, which was sometimes paid in kind. Two 'roody-bakers' (turnips) or two eggs for one penny, or a quarter of a pound of cream for twopence were considered fair exchange.

> She (the Dame) sat in a big arm-chair with her feet on a 'tut' (hassock), from which point of vantage she could go on with her

Final stages of construction in these knit-frocks, showing the skills of two young Polperro girls.

11

knitting, take snuff at intervals and keep an eye on her charges... In the afternoons, while the boys did knitting, the girls did sewing and wool work.   PAYNTER, *History of St. Ives**

In 1818 a distress situation was declared on the Isles of Scilly, owing to severe weather and bad seasons, and public support was organised from the mainland. In 1819, a fishing industry was established, and at the same time, a School of Industry for the Scilly Isles was formed, 'to employ all those widows, infirm and aged women and distressed orphans, whom the fisheries could not relieve'. The female committee taught straw-plait; widows and children knitted stockings; fourteen girls from Newlyn and Mousehole were placed on the Islands to instruct in braiding nets; and a woman from Essex was sent, with a new spinning wheel, to instruct in 'spinning, with both hands, shoe-thread and line twine'.

On 27 August, the following advertisement appeared in the *West Briton*:

The Committee of the Society respectfully acquaint the public that they have constantly on sale, at their depot in Penzance, a variety of goods, manufactured by the poor of Scilly – viz. –

Worsted and Lamb's Wool STOCKINGS,
Men's Worsted and Yarn FROCKS,
Cotton Gloves, and Men's BRACES,
Children's SOCKS, in Wool and Cotton,
Fine, and Coarse STRAW-PLAT,
Men's Summer STRAW-HATS,
Shoemaker's THREAD,
Ladies' small fancy Articles in
WORK-BAGS, NOTE-CASES, PINCUSHIONS, etc.

The Prince Regent, Duke of Cornwall, accepted the office of patron and was duly honoured with a gift of two pairs of lambswool stockings, knitted by two of the islanders. His initials, G.P.R., were neatly wrought in crimson silk, surrounded with a fanciful wreath, on each stocking.

As had happened earlier on in the Channel Islands, the hand-knitting industry throughout Cornwall developed, and local sources of wool became inadequate. Yorkshire, in the industrial north, was at the centre of speedy developments in machine-spinning, and soon supplied yarn to wholesale distributors in the Channel Islands, Devon and Cornwall, as well as the east and north-east of England. Some of these trading links, started early in the nineteenth century, lasted well into the twentieth century.

---

* The schoolmistress was often the handywoman of the village, eking out her living by knitting or patching and mending clothes for her neighbours, so that at times she would be too busy to teach.

Contract Knitters

Lee, R.H. and Co., of 16 and 18 Fore St., St. Austell and at Liskeard:
agents for Hand-knit guernsey frocks.

Kelly's Directory, 1893

Throughout the nineteenth century, large numbers of Cornishmen left their home county to seek their fortunes elsewhere. Local newspapers published information about new opportunities overseas, and agencies offered incentives to potential emigrants in the form of assisted passages to Novia Scotia, Western Australia, Queensland and New Zealand, for work in mining or agriculture. Free land was sometimes an additional bonus. The gold rush to Australia in the 1850s and mining developments in South Africa in the 1880s also attracted many Cornishmen.

To avoid an arduous journey by road, travellers from the far west made their way to Hayle where a regular paddle-steamer service operated to Bristol. The boats generally left Hayle at about 3 o'clock in the afternoon (if the tide was right) and after a frequently rough journey, arrived at Bristol the next morning. Thence passengers continued their journey by road, rail or sea. From 1859, when the first train thundered over Brunel's new railway bridge at Saltash, Cornish people enjoyed improved communications and travel facilities.

Knitting became a necessary and available occupation for many women, for both financial and social reasons. By 1901, with a population of 322,334 declared in the offical census, 6,434 were wives whose husbands were at sea, or working abroad, and often the women bore the financial burden of the children.

Agents, merchants and wholesalers played important roles in the organisation of home industries. Knitters and other home-workers in a community usually worked under contract to an agent, and his visit once a week or once a month became an important occasion. He brought fresh supplies of yarn, inspected and collected the completed work, made the payments and arranged the next stage of marketing.

Many home knitters took their work to a local shop or agency, and payment was received in cash or kind. One Looe shopkeeper was renowned for 'breaking every Truck Law in the book': she insisted that all her knitters were paid with goods from the shop and absolutely refused to make cash payments.

In October 1859, J. Elliot, a draper of Liskeard, advertised in the local paper:

Wanted, immediately, 100 Hands to Knit Frocks.
They must be quite competent to undertake the work.

Knitting became a necessary occupation for many women whose husbands were away and who often bore the financial burden of the children. Mrs. Jane Jolliff in her accustomed 'knitting place' at Polperro.

13

In October 1869, Bowden's the drapers, of Looe, required:

500 good Frock Knitters,
constant employment.

Richard Poppleton's of Wakefield, Yorkshire, the manufacturers of yarn fo[r] guernseys, have records of supplying the wholesalers Messrs. Tippett and Sons o[f] Plymouth in 1883. Tippett's in turn, supplied Mr. Tom Bowden's shop at Looe[.] Guernseys were still being knitted by contract workers for Bowden's in the 1920[s] and 1930s.

Mr. Broad of Liskeard was another local agent well-remembered in the area. Hi[s] draper's shop existed from the 1860s into this century.* 'Mr. R.K.' travelled fron[m] Liskeard to Looe by train once a week to supervise collections of work. At St. Cleer[,] a village on Caradon Moor, a Mr. Fox came once a week 'in a pony and trap', as M[r] Broad's agent.

Much of the knitting was done out of doors, and there were recognised place[s] where women met to work:

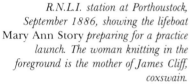

R.N.L.I. station at Porthoustock, September 1886, showing the lifeboat Mary Ann Story *preparing for a practice launch. The woman knitting in the foreground is the mother of James Cliff, coxswain.*

In Newlyn, a great deal of gossiping on summer evenings goes on around the small wells, whilst the women wait patiently for each in turn to fill her earthen pitcher; some of the most industrious bring their knitting in their pockets with them.

COURTNEY, *Cornish Feasts and Folklore*

Polperro women knitting 'up at Pig's House' during the Second World War. This was a favourite knitting and meeting place for more than 100 years.

In St. Ives, the 'Ca'astle' was a regular venue. This was situated between the Island and the quay and was formerly a stone embattlement or platform for a few heavy guns. In Polperro, women knitted 'up at Pig's house' along the cliff path, or at the 'Peak', where the rocks tower high over the harbour. They knitted as they walked or talked, stood at cottage doors or watched events of general interest.

In Looe, knitters regularly organised collections of guernseys from their group, packing about eight or ten each upon their backs. They walked over the cliffs to Plymouth – 'about twelve miles, if you know the short cuts' – to deliver them to 'W. Johns and Co., General Drapers in Old Town Street', and other agents. They walked in their 'pattins', a sort of wooden clog with an iron rim at the bottom which raised their feet an inch or an inch and a half from the ground, to protect them from the wet. They knitted all the way, often pinning an extra skein of yarn to their skirts, 'so they would never run out'. On their return journey, they brought fresh supplies of yarn.

With large families and limited resources, many knitters devised their own

* In 1971, in Liskeard, I met a lady of seventy-five who had been employed as one of Mr. Broad's packers when she left school. It was her job to pack the knitting 'for export'. When I asked the destination, she replied, Great Yarmouth!

15

'The Boy Musicians': home-made entertainment in Polperro. Knit-frocks reaching almost to the knee and thick stockings in 'hobbies' (hob-nailed boots) were regular gear for small children. The two designs at the back show intricate pattern detail.

methods of economy. 'Contract' guernseys were sometimes 'damped down and put under a cushion' or 'put through the mangle', to stretch them a bit. With oddments of yarn squeezed from their consignments, they knitted stockings for the children, often with striped effects from the use of different dye-lots. Any guernseys made for their children were big enough to 'grow into' and often came down to the knee. Wholesalers were undoubtedly aware of these schemes, and, now and again, would check the completed garments by weight to ensure that the correct amount of yarn had been used.

In the warehouse, there was usually a 'worsted room', piled ceiling-high with brown paper packages of yarn and guernseys. This was the scene of the final stages of the local contract knitting industry. Girls were employed to pack the completed garments for dispatch to their ultimate destinations and fresh yarn was received to start the cycle again.

Sticks and Needles

I must not forget to mention that tied round her waist was a wooden fish, in the open mouth of which the end of one of her busy knitting needles rested.

PAYNTER, *History of St. Ives*

Speed and accuracy were all-important to knitters who were producing guernseys and stockings under contract, or for sale at fairs and markets.

The use of a holder to anchor the 'working' needle in circular knitting allowed the knitter greater freedom in throwing the loops over the head of the needle, increased the pace of the work and improved the tension. It became a specialised technique adopted by most traditional knitters.

The holder was basically a piece of hardwood, eight or nine inches (20-23cm) long, shaped like a prong or fork, or like a single arm. It curved slightly at the lower end to lie comfortably over the hip, and was hooked over or into a waistband, belt, length of 'inkle' tape or ribbon (string was not used, because it would cut into the wearer). If the knitter preferred, it could be tucked under the arm. A fine hole for a specific size of needle was pierced about two inches (5cm) into the narrow end of the stick. This served as a socket for the 'working' needle in a set of from four to seven needles.

Freed from the necessity to hold the working needle, the knitter could use the

Two examples of knitting sticks from St. Ives, known locally as 'knitting fish'. These had carved slits, to fit over a belt or waistband.

17

fingers of the right hand as a shuttle to move the stitches from the left-hand needle. This greatly increased the speed of knitting and by a rhythmical motion of arms and body, the knitter would strike the loops 'faster than the eye could see'. Experienced knitters achieved very high speeds of about 200 stitches a minute!

> 'fingers like wizard's' (Miss Jordan, St. Keverne)
>
> 'Granny's fingers moved so fast, you couldn't see them'
> (Mrs. Edmunds, St. Blazey)
>
> 'fingers going all blue at the ends' (St. Ive)

Mr. Nicholas of West Looe recalled the distinctive clacking noise of needles struck at speed, which could be heard 'before you turned the street corner'.

Wooden sticks or sheaths were often given as tokens of affection by young men to their sweethearts, and as with lace bobbins, Welsh loving spoons and similar tokens, hearts were favourite emblems in their decoration. Initials and dates were sometimes carved. The earliest local example recorded is 'E.M. 1844', on a stick made for Elizabeth Moyse of North Hill near Launceston. Rough chip carving, executed with a penknife, produced simple designs and markings which were quite individual. The examples found in Cornwall are comparatively modest in carving skill and decoration, but have nevertheless been treasured by families for many years.

Miss Spear of Callington and Mrs. Sleep of Bolventor have knitting sticks carved by their grandfathers for their grandmothers; Mrs. Hoskins of Liskeard has a knitting 'arm' in elder used one hundred years ago. Mr. Harding of Liskeard made a stick for me as his wife remembered them being made in her childhood. He selected a forked elder twig from the hedgerow, stripped the bark, and made the socket with a red-hot skewer.

Three examples from St. Ives, used by the Hawken and Wedge families, were always known as 'knitting fish'. A Polperro stick was carved from wood from the wreck of the Danish schooner *Neilson* in 1926, when a local boy, Joseph Curtis, was honoured by the R.N.L.I. for his bravery in the rescue of one of the crew.

Metal was an uncommon material for holders, but a wooden stick carved from an old chair leg and found in Millbrook, had a brass 'eye' screwed to the socket. Charles Nicholas remembers his grandmother using one 'made out of a flat piece of brass about the size of an old five-shilling piece with a piece of copper pipe soldered on to hold the needle. The flat round of brass had two holes in it with two pieces of tape threaded through'.

Cornish knitting sticks. The one on the left is carved with the date and initials, 'E.M. 1844', for Elizabeth Moyse of North Hill.

Other holders familiar to Cornish knitters were:

> a hollow tube, *e.g.* bamboo (Camelford)
> a leather 'tack' (Port Isaac)
> a velvet pad (St. Ives)
> 'like a pincushion, kidney-shaped, stuffed
>   with straw or hay' (St. Keverne)
> 'a wad of straw stuffed into a sock and tucked
>   into the apron waistband' (Portscatho)
> a tight twist of straw (Hayle).

Elsewhere in the British Isles, knitters used holders of wood as well as other materials: bundles of feathers tightly bound were recorded in the north of Scotland; a leather pouch, stuffed with horsehair and perforated with holes for the needles, in the Shetland Islands, and bundles of fine sticks sewn into a linen bag and called 'bundly sticks' in Northumberland.

Museums in Yorkshire and the north-east of England have fine collections of knitting sticks and sheaths, reflecting the important contribution made by knitters in this area to the hand-knitting industry over the past 150 years. Many sticks are beautiful examples of craftsmanship with intricate carving and unusual decoration. Bone, silver and ivory were sometimes used, but examples of these are mainly found on the continent. One from France, dating from the seventeenth century, is housed at the County Museum in Truro.

Knitting needles used for traditional guernseys were made of steel,[*] pointed at both ends, and about fourteen inches (36 cm) long. They were purchased in sets of five. Everyone who remembers this type of knitting, mentions that the needles were 'very fine', with size 16 (1½mm) being specified at Mevagissey! Difficulty in obtaining needles during the First World War led to interesting improvisations: a set was fashioned from bicycle spokes at St. Columb (Mrs. Osborne) and from umbrella spokes at Millbrook (Miss Bartlett).

Sets of long stocking needles are still manufactured, but are now made of anodised aluminium and are less rigid than the steel ones. They can be purchased (in sets of four) in a few specialised shops. Contemporary knitters may prefer to use a circular needle or twin-pin which is readily available and light and easy to use. Traditions die hard, however, and Mrs. Wiscombe (who is eighty-six) of Bodmin, an authentic knitter of guernseys, says, 'I use the long stocking needles, as I believe it is not correct to use a circular one'.

---

[*] 'A steel knitting needle held downwards between the teeth when peeling onions prevents the eyes watering' – an unusual household hint from the *Cornish Times* in 1901.

A knitting stick from Looe, with its original tapes, by which it was tied around the waist of the knitter.

19

Polperro

3, Bevil's Row, Jane Pinch, 19, Knitter of Frocks.
41, Talland Street, Susanna White, 65, Knitter.
101, Warren, Rebecca Langmaid, 11, Knitter.

1851 Census

Women's hands were never idle as they stood at 'the Peak'. This woman is using a knitting stick (note the position of the fingers); the bulk of knitting is pinned to her waistband, and her ball of wool is spiked on the railings. Polperro, 1904.

The fishing industry employed many men at sea and many more, with women and children, in allied occupations – salting, pressing, bulking, cleaning and washing the fish and making boats, nets, ropes and casks. Most residents in Polperro were directly involved in this kind of work. There were periods of frenzied activity when every available hand was needed, and quieter times of waiting and hoping for work and wages.

Knitting was an occupation which suited local women well. Their hands were never idle as they stood at 'the Peak' looking out for signs of shoals of fish, or the

return of the boats, or watching the landing and weighing on the quay.

Children became involved as soon as they were old enough to handle the needles, although the weight of the knitting prevented them from being too ambitious. One old lady recalled, 'There were nine maids in our family; the little ones knitted the 'trails', the bigger maids knitted the plain bits and Mother did the pattern.' The 'trails' were the ribs at the beginning of the work and this section was not too cumbersome or heavy for little fingers.

At the beginning of this century, women were paid 3s. 6d. (17½ pence) for a

The quay, Polperro, always busy at the weigh-in of the catch. Knitting women and girls were a familiar part of the scene.

The famous panel of 82 photographs in the Rowett Institute, Polperro. The photographs were taken in the late nineteenth century and all are named.

'fancy' knit-frock; 2s. 6d. (12½ pence) or 2s. 9d. (14 pence) for a plain one. An eighty-year-old lady pointed out that only 2s. (10 pence) was paid if a fault were found in the knitting. The yarn was received in 2lb. (900g) hanks (cost 4s. [20 pence]) and was wound by the knitters. An experienced contract worker could complete a guernsey in about a week. Comparative wages in the late nineteenth century were 'Bal maidens* at £10 – £11 per year; a 'thoroughly competent and experienced woman servant at £8 per year', and 'domestic servants at 9d. (about 4 pence) a week'. The latter were known as 'ninepennies'.

* 'Bal maidens' were employed as surface workers at Cornish mines to do the heavy work of 'spalling' or breaking large rocks with long-handled hammers, prior to the dressing of tin with copper ores.

Richard Searle of Polperro in his knit-frock. The fine pattern detail still stands out, more than 100 years after the photograph was taken.

In the official census of 1851, twenty-eight women and girls from Polperro were listed as 'knitters'.

The village is unique in its record of knitting history. Not only was it a source of contract knitters for more than a century, but it was the temporary home of a remarkable exponent of the art of photography from the early years of its development. Lewis Harding left a distinguished photographic record from the 1850s which illustrates a wide variety of designs and skill in the craft of knitting. In the Rowett Institute hangs a panel of photographs of eighty-two Polperro fishermen of the 1860s. Each is named and wears a knit-frock. About fifteen men wear the 'seeds and bars' pattern and others wear 'ribs'. A few wear more intricate patterns.

Elsewhere in the village, old family photographs have been retrieved and studied. They all reflect the skilled knitting techniques of Polperro women over more than a hundred years.

Cornish
Patterns

'Make the rope tight or
'e w'a'n't stand out.'
William Stephens

RIGHT
A fisherman at Porthgwarra.

OPPOSITE
L. to R.: W. Nicholls, Captain Martin and
J. Bath. Captain Martin of the Bude ketch
President Garfield *was presented with*
this walnut clock in recognition of his
gallantry in the rescue of 2 Boscastle
fishermen in 1906.

Guernsey knitting, unless under contract, was a labour of love, demanding skill, patience and the best materials that could be afforded. Garments were made to last and often lasted more than twenty years. The deep indigo dye of the first knitting gradually faded in the light and the salty air, to a lighter navy, through a shade of purple to green and grey, colours that correspond vividly to those of the Cornish sea in all its various moods and seasons.

Fishermen and other men of the sea wore their guernseys on all occasions:

> 'All my brothers wore them. They were coastguards and used to go to France for produce.' (St. Keverne)

> 'All these men were pilots and the crew of a pilot cutter of Trinity House known as No. 5 Ferret.' (Cawsand)

> 'George Henry Johnson wore that guernsey for as long as I can remember, whenever he was on beach patrol at Bude.'

George Henry Johnson on bathing patrol at Bude.

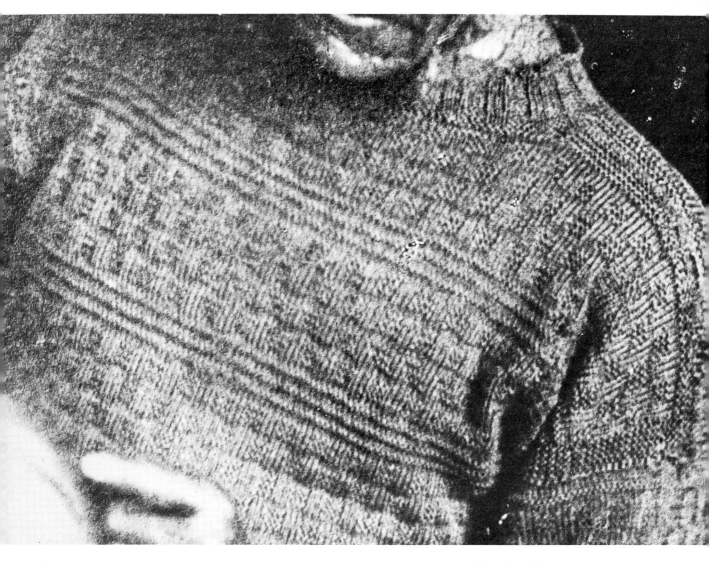

The first Cornish guernsey pattern was recorded directly from an old photograph of 1872, lent by Mr. T. Hart of the Lizard. The matt brownish surface retained clear detail of the knitting and it was possible to read the stitches with the naked eye. The task of relating these stitches to actual knitting tension proved much more difficult.

Background study of guernsey knitting from the Channel Islands and all parts of

A closer view of the lattice pattern from the Lizard. 1872.

the British Isles helped to establish the average tension required. This, co-ordinated with the stitches seen in the photograph, revealed that what at first sight appeared to be a block of 3 plain and 3 purl stitches, was in fact 3 plain and 3 garter stitches. The inserted plain rows allowed the surface tension to rise and fall gently rather than dramatically, and the resultant pattern gave the effect of a woven lattice rather than alternate blocks.

The second pattern was also recorded from the Lizard. The late Mr. Willie Stephens, who was chief mechanic of the Lizard lifeboat, had knitted guernseys all

Mr. Willie Stephens, chief mechanic of the Lizard lifeboat, knitted guernseys all his life.

his life from a memorised pattern. When he was a boy, his school teacher used to cast on the stitches for him.

The guernsey he wore in the photograph showed ten cable panels across the front yoke, and his only advice was, 'Make the rope tight or 'e w'a'n't stand out'. In preparing the knitting sample and chart, it was necessary first to establish the number of stitches in each panel, then the frequency of the twist. Stitches twisted too frequently caused a 'drag' across the work and holes at each side; stitches twisted infrequently resulted in a flat area between the twists. A piece of rope is twisted in an even spiral throughout its length and this proved the right formula to make the cable 'stand out' from the seeding background, just as Mr. Stephens had

Photographic records have proved the most accurate source of patterns. Govier of Falmouth, Preston of Penzance, Gibson of the Isles of Scilly and Thorne of Bude were four of the early Cornish photographers whose work involved men of the sea. Most photographs are still in private homes, in old albums, boxes, drawers and attics, and a few which have been located have revealed pattern interest.

From Bude, four separate knitting patterns were identified when a large collection of photographs was being assembled for the opening of the Bude Historical Folk Exhibition* in 1976.

The first pattern was of seeds and bars, as found elsewhere in the county and country. The next was seen on a mural at the Falcon Inn – this was a ladder pattern created by a simple geometric arrangement of plain and garter stitches.

George Bate, listed in the Parish Register as a 'mariner', was a member of the crew of the hobble boat** at Bude in the 1860s and was famous for a rescue for which he was awarded a gold medal. He wore his guernsey with a smart cravat and waistcoat. The same knitting design was being used at Sennen Cove fifty years later. (See p.5.)

Robert Stephen Hawker, vicar of Morwenstow until his death in 1875, was

ABOVE LEFT
George Bate of Bude wore his guernsey with a smart cravat and waistcoat. 1860.
ABOVE RIGHT
Reverend Robert Stephen Hawker, Vicar of Morwenstow 1834-75, wearing a guernsey patterned in an interesting variation of basket stitch.

---

* now permanently housed at the Old Forge, by the Bude Canal.

** a hobble boat is used for general work around a port, for instance assisting ships by taking aboard hawsers when they come in to port, and taking visitors boating, rather than for fishing or trading.

LEFT
William Henry Laity of Porthleven, who was drowned at sea in the 1880s. Photograph by Govier. 1880.

RIGHT
Thomas Henry Nicholas, coxswain of the Sennen Cove lifeboat and 61 times afloat on service. This photograph was taken by Preston of Penzance in 1921.

photographed in two different designs – one a rib and one an interesting variation of basket stitch. Blocks of 8 plain stitches and 4 garters alternate, with a single garter line between. The closer tension of the garter stitch blocks creates a wave in the garter line, which is complemented at the next block.

Govier's photograph, dating from 1880, is of William Henry Laity of Porthleven who was drowned at sea when he was a young man. Variations of rib widths were used for different sizes, with the main panel remaining the same.

The R.N.L.I. Museum at Poole in Dorset houses a fine collection of reference material relating to all lifeboat stations, past and present, around the coasts of Great Britain. Two photographs taken by Preston of Penzance in 1920, show Sennen Cove lifeboatmen wearing patterned guernseys under their gear.

Looe, St. Ives, the Isles of Scilly and Port Isaac boast hundreds and thousands of photographs connected with the sea, in both private collections and public exhibitions. None, however, contained sufficient close-up detail from which to record patterns, but in the course of the search other sources of information presented themselves.

Cornish Patterns : Knitting Instructions

The patterns that follow may be used with the basic guernsey pattern given on pp. 63-5.

1 The Lizard: Lattice

51 rounds

Round 1: P.
St.-st. 4 rounds.
Repeat these 5 rounds twice.
Round 16: P.3, K.3 to end.
Rounds 17 and 19: K.
Rounds 18 and 20: As 16th.
St.-st. 4 rounds.
Rounds 25, 27 and 29: K.3, P.3 to end.
Rounds 26 and 28: K.
St.-st. 4 rounds.
Rounds 34-38: As 16th.-20th.
St.-st. 4 rounds.
Rounds 43-47: As 25th.-29th.
St.-st. 4 rounds.

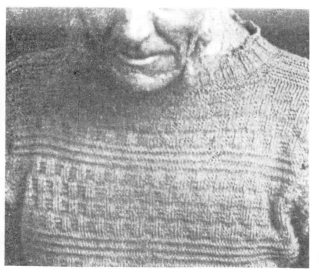

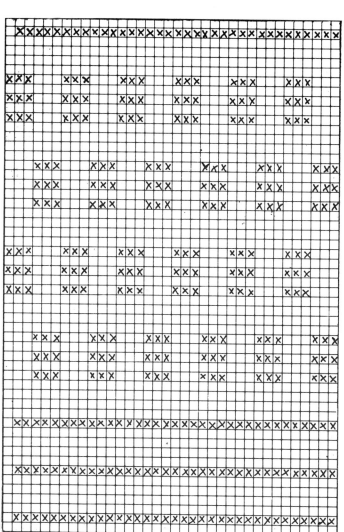

2 The Vicar of Morwenstow: Slate

28 rounds

Round 1: P.
Round 2 and alternate rounds: K.
Round 3: K.6, (P.4, K.8) to end.
Rounds 5, 7, 9, 11 and 13: As 3rd.
Round 15: P.
Round 17: (P.4, K.8) to end.
Rounds 19, 21, 23, 25 and 27: As 17th.

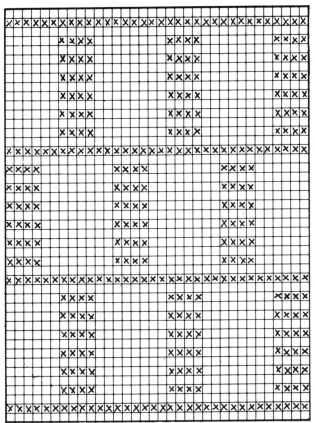

3 Bude: Ladder

12 rounds

Round 1 and every alternate round: K.
Round 2: P.
Round 4: K.3, (P.1, K.11) to end.
Rounds 6, 8, 10 and 12: As 4th.

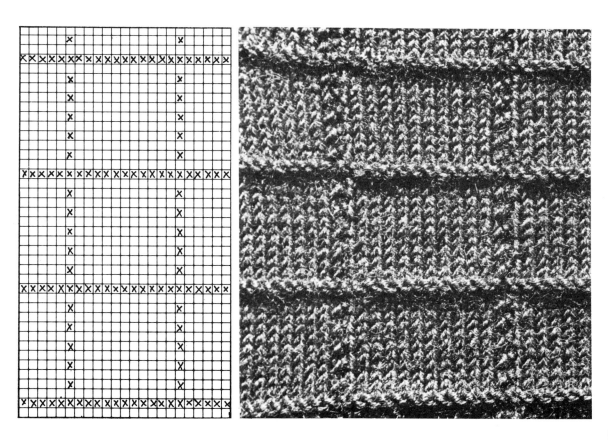

4 The Lizard, William Stephens: Rope

8 rounds

Round 1: K.2 (P.1, K.8) to end.
Round 2: K.2 (K.10, P.2, K.2, P.2, K.2) to end.
Round 3: As 1st.
Round 4: P.2 (K.12, K.2, P.2, K.2, P.2) to end.
Round 5: K.2 (P.1, slip 4 sts. on to cable needle and leave at back, K.4 from L.-H. needle, K.4 from cable needle, P.1, K.8) to end.
Round 6: As 2nd.
Round 7: As 1st.
Round 8: As 4th.

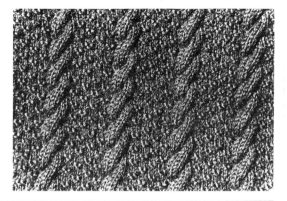

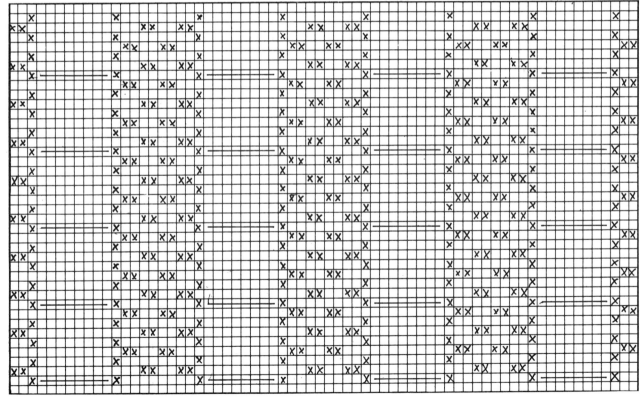

5 Looe: Eddystone

14 rounds

Round 1 and alternate rounds: K.
Round 2: (P.7, K.4) to end.
Round 4: K.1 (P.5, K.6) to end.
Round 6: K.2 (P.3, K.8) to end.
Round 8: K.3 (P.1, K.10) to end.
Round 10: As 8th.
St.-st. 4 rounds.

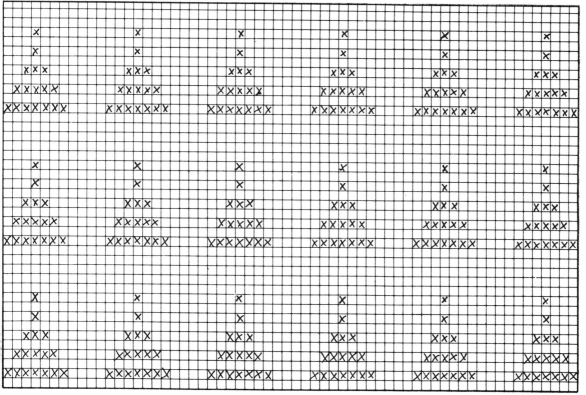

6 Bude, George Bate: Hobble

16 rounds

Round 1 and alternate rounds: K.
Round 2 and alternate rounds: (P.2, K.12, P.2, K.6) to end.
Round 7 and every following 16th round: CABLE thus: (K.2, slip 6 sts
    on to cable needle and leave at the back of the work, K. the
    next 6 sts., then K. the 6 sts. from the cable needle, K.2, K.6).
    Repeat to end.

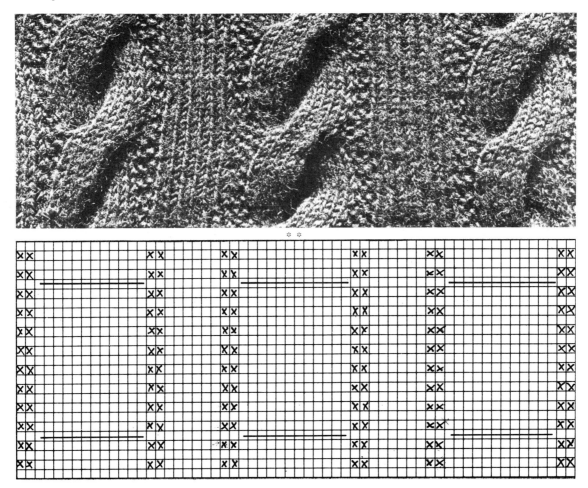

7 Port Isaac: Double Rope

16 rounds

This pattern is planned in 5 sections: two panels of 'double rope' over 26 sts. with seeding on three sides to desired width.

SEEDING: *Round 1 and every alternate round (except cable rounds):* K.
Round 2: K.2, P.2 to end of section 1; K.12, P.2, K.12; P.2, K.2 to end.
Round 4: P.2, K.2 to end of section 1; K.12, P.2, K.12; K.2, P.2 to end.

MAIN PANEL: This is cabled on the 15th. and every following 16th. round thus: *Slip the next 6sts. on to a cable needle and leave at the back of work; K.6 sts. from the L.-H. needle, knit the 6 sts. from the cable needle*, K.2, repeat from * to * once.

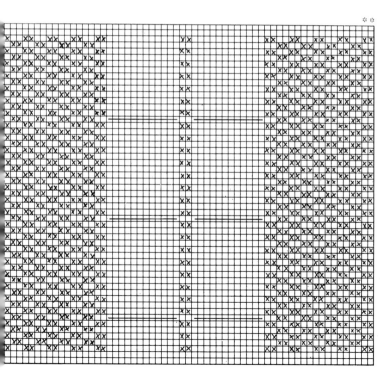 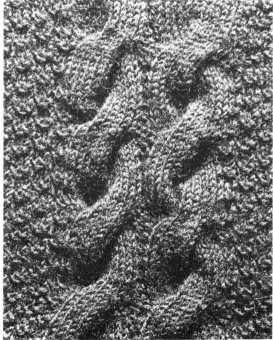

8 St. Ives: background slip-stitch

2-round repeat

Round 1: P.
Round 2: (K.1, slip 1 purlwise). Repeat to end.

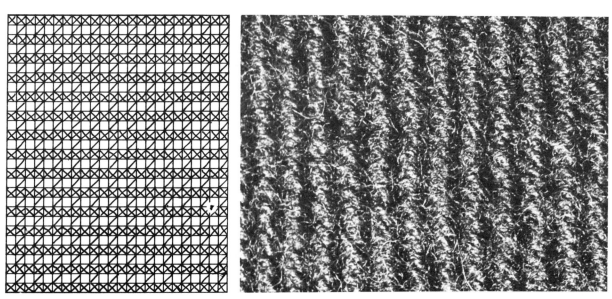

9 St. Ives: Double Twist

rounds

LL ROUNDS KNIT with cables on every 4th. round.
ound 3: (K.2, slip the next 4 sts. on to cable needle and leave at
    front, K.4, K.4 from cable needle, K.4). Repeat to end.
ound 7: (K.6, slip the next 4 sts. on to cable needle and leave at
    front, K.4, K.4 from cable needle). Repeat to end.

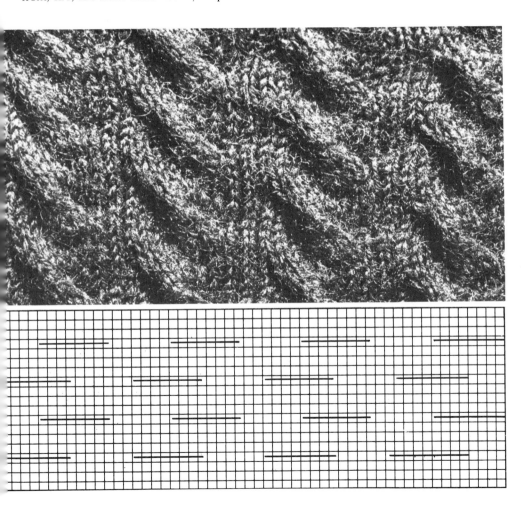

10 Sennen Cove

24 rounds

Round 1: (K.10; K.6, P.1, K.6; K.10; cable 8 F). Repeat to end.
Round 2: (P.2, K.2, P.2, K.2, P.2; K.5, moss 3, K.5; P.2, K.2, P.2, K.2, P.2; K.8). Repeat to end.
Round 3: (K.10; K.4, moss 5, K.4; K.10; K.8). Repeat to end.
Round 4: (Rib 10; K.3, moss 7, K.3; rib 10; K.8). Repeat to end.
Round 5: (K.10; K.2, moss 9, K.3; K.10; K.8). Repeat to end.
Round 6: (Rib 10; K.1, moss 11, K.1; rib 10; K.8). Repeat to end.
Round 7: (K.10; K.2, moss 9, K.2; K.10; K.8). Repeat to end.
Round 8: (Rib 10; K.3, moss 7, K.3; rib 10; K.8). Repeat to end.
Round 9: (K.10; K.4, moss 5, K.4; K.10; cable 8 F). Repeat to end.
Round 10: (Rib 10; K.5, moss 3, K.5; rib 10; K.8). Repeat to end.
Round 11: (K.10; K.6, P.1, K.6; K.10; K.8). Repeat to end.
Round 12: (Rib 10; K. 13; rib 10; K.8). Repeat to end.
Rounds 13 and 15: K.
Rounds 14, 16, 18, 20, 22 and 24: As 12th.
Round 17: (K.10; K.13; K.10; cable 8 F). Repeat to end.
Rounds 19, 21, 23: K.

OR

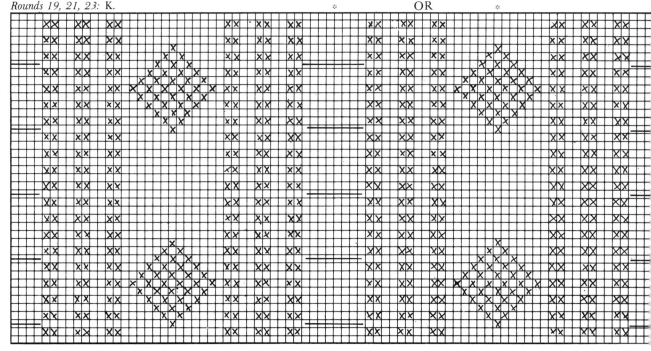

40

1 Isles of Scilly

rounds

rounds 1 and 3: K.
round 2 and alternate rounds: (P.3, sl.1 knitwise, P.3, sl.1 knitwise,
    P.3, K.8, repeat to end.
round 5: K.11, cable 8 F. Repeat to end.
round 7: K.

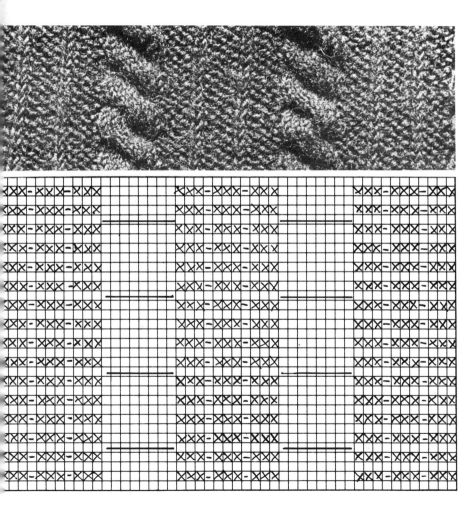

12   Porthleven

20 rounds

3 sections.

Round 1: (K.3, P.3), repeat; K.19; (P.3, K.3) to end.
Round 2: K; K.9, P.1, K.9; K. to end.
Round 3: (K.3, P.3), repeat; K.8, P.1, K.1, P.1, K.8; (P.3, K.3) to end.
Round 4: K; K.7, P.1, K.3, P.1, K.7; K. to end.
Round 5: (K.3, P.3), repeat; K.6, P.1, K.5, P.1, K.6; (P.3, K.3) to end.
Round 6: K; K.5, P.1, K.7, P.1, K.5; K. to end.

Round 7: (K.3, P.3), repeat; K.4, P.1, K.9, P.1, K.4; (P.3, K.3) to en
Round 8: K; K.3, P.1, K.11, P.1, K.3; K. to end.
Round 9: (K.3, P.3), repeat; K.2, P.1, K.13, P.1, K.2; (P.3, K.3)
   to end.
Round 10: K; K.1, P.1, K.15, P.1, K.1; K. to end.

Work 10 rounds with centre panel in st.-st. and 3 x 3 rib at side

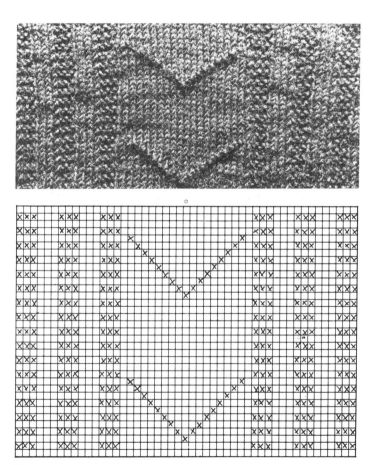

13(a) Polperro: Seeds and Bars
2 rounds

Round 1: P.
Rounds 2-4: K.
Repeat these 4 rounds twice.
Round 13: P. Knit the next 2 rounds.
Round 16: (K.2, P.2) to end.
Round 17 and alternate rounds: K.
Round 18: (P.2, K.2) to end.
Rounds 20, 24 and 28: (K.2, P.2) to end.
Rounds 22, 26 and 30: (P.2, K.2) to end.
Knit 2 rounds.

13(b) Polperro: Seeds and Bars
24 rounds

Round 1: P.
Rounds 2-4: K.
Repeat these 4 rounds once.
Round 9: P. Knit the next 2 rounds.
Round 12: (K.2, P.2) to end.
Round 13 and alternate rounds: K.
Round 14: (P.2, K.2) to end.
Rounds 16 and 20: As 12th.
Rounds 18 and 22: As 14th.
Rounds 23 and 24: K.

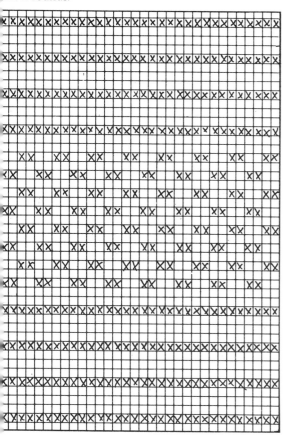

14 Polperro: Jack Searle

40 rounds

Round 1 and alternate rounds: K.
Rounds 2 and 4: P.1, K.3, P.1 (K.22, P.2, K.22, P.1, K.3, P.1) to end.
Rounds 6 and 8: P.1, K.3, P.1 (K.20, P.2, K.2, P.2, K.20, P.1, K.3, P.1) to end.
Rounds 10 and 12: P.1, K.3, P.1 (K.18, P.2 [K.2, P.2] twice, K.18, P.1, K.3, P.1) to end.
Rounds 14 and 16: P.1, K.3, P.1 (K.16, P.2 [K.2, P.2] x 3, K.16, P.1, K.3, P.1) to end.
Rounds 18 and 20: P.1, K.3, P.1 (K.14, P.2 [K.2, P.2] x 4, K.14, P.1, K.3, P.1) to end.

Rounds 22 and 24: P.1, K.3, P.1 (K.12, P.2 [K.2, P.2] x 5, K.12, P.1, K.3, P.1) to end.
Rounds 26 and 28: P.1, K.3, P.1 (K.10, P.2 [K.2, P.2] x 6, K.10, P.1, K.3, P.1) to end.
Rounds 30 and 32: P.1, K.3, P.1 (K.8, P.2 [K.2, P.2] x 7, K.8, P.1, K.3, P.1) to end.
Rounds 34 and 36: P.1, K.3, P.1 (K.6, P.2 [K.2, P.2] x 8, K.6, P.1, K.3, P.1) to end.
Rounds 38 and 40: P.1, K.3, P.1 (K.4, P.2 [K.2, P.2] x 9, K.4, P.1, K.3, P.1) to end.

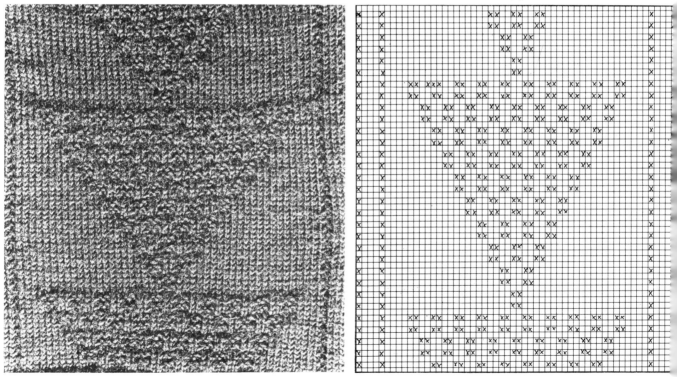

44

15 Polperro: Vertical Diamonds

16 rounds

Round 1: (Moss 2, K.1, moss 2, K.9, P.1, K.9) to end.
Round 2: (Moss 2, K.1, moss 2, K.8, P.1, K.1, P.1, K.8) to end.
Round 3: (Moss 2, K.1, moss 2, K.7, P.1, K.1, P.1, K.1, P.1, K.7)
    to end.
Round 4: (Moss 2, K.1, moss 2, K.6, P.1, K.5, P.1, K.6) to end.
Round 5: (Moss 2, K.1, moss 2, K.5, P.1, K.3, P.1, K.3, P.1, K.5)
    to end.
Round 6: (Moss 2, K.1, moss 2, K.4, P.1, K.9, P.1, K.4) to end.
Round 7: (Moss 2, K.1, moss 2, K.3, P.1, K.5, P.1, K.5, P.1, K.3)
    to end.
Round 8: (Moss 2, K.1, moss 2, K.2, P.1, K.13, P.1, K.2) to end.
Round 9: (Moss 2, K.1, moss 2, K.1, P.1, K.7, P.1, K.7, P.1, K.1)
    to end.
Rounds 10-16: As rounds 8-2 in reverse order.

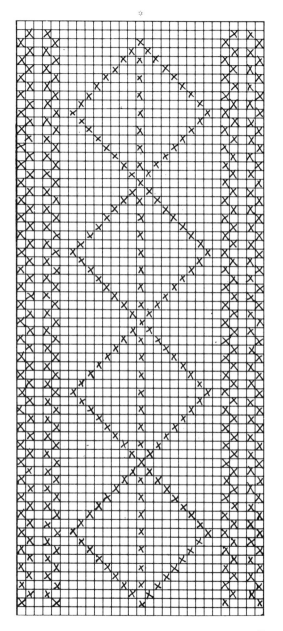

16 Polperro: Northcott

RIB BAND: 2-round repeat:

Round 1: K.
Round 2: K.4, P.2.
　　　　Beginning with a K. round, work 22 rounds O.R.L.

GARTER BAND: 6-round repeat:

Round 1: K.
Round 2: P.
Rounds 3-5: K.
Round 6: P.

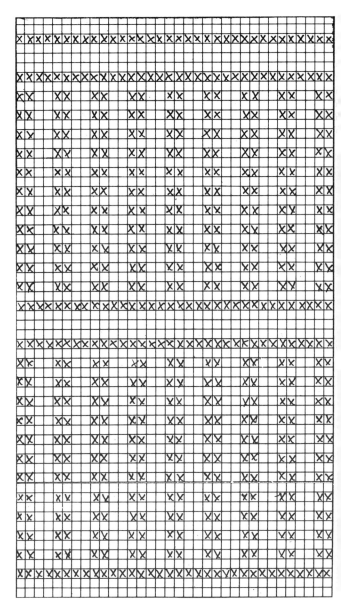

17 Polperro: Musician

8 rounds

Round 1: (K.2, P.2, K.2;P.1, K.7, P.1, K.7, P.1) to end.
Round 2: (K.6;   K.7, P.1, K.1, P.1, K.7) to end.
Round 3: (P.2, K.2, P.2;K.6, P.1, K.3, P.1, K.6) to end.
Round 4: (K.6;   K.5, P.1, K.5, P.1, K.5) to end
Round 5: (K.2, P.2, K.2;K.4, P.1, K.7, P.1, K.4) to end.
Round 6: (K.6;   K.3, P.1, K.9, P.1, K.3) to end.
Round 7: (P.2, K.2, P.2;K.2, P.1, K.11, P.1, K.2) to end.
Round 8: (K.6;   K.1, P.1, K.13, P.1, K.1) to end.

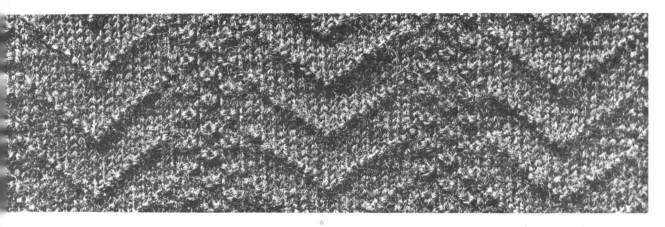

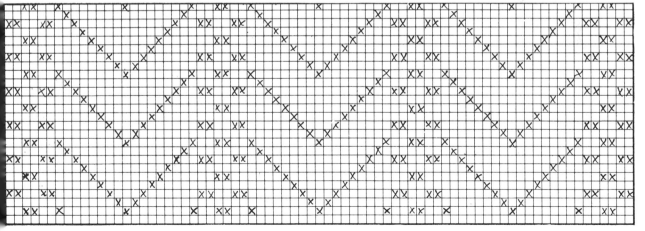

18 Polperro: Laughing Boy

8 rounds

4 rounds st.-st.
Round 5: K.
Round 6: (K.4, P.2). Repeat to end.
Rounds 7 and 8: As 5 and 6.

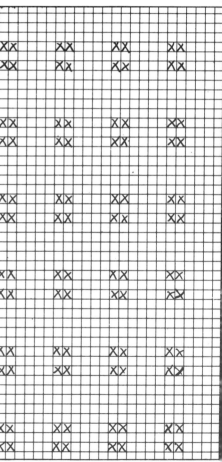

19 Polperro: Moss Diamonds

18 rounds

Round 1: (P.3; K.19) Repeat to end.
Round 2: (K.3; K.9, P.1, K.9) to end.
Round 3: (P.3; K.8, moss 3, K.8) to end.
Round 4: (K.3; K.7, moss 5, K.7) to end.
Round 5: (P.3; K.6, moss 7, K.6) to end.
Round 6: (K.3; K.5, moss 9, K.5) to end.
Round 7: (P.3; K.4, moss 11, K.4) to end.
Round 8: (K.3; K.3, moss 13, K.3) to end.
Round 9: (P.3; K.2, moss 15, K.2) to end.
Round 10: (K.3; K.1, moss 17, K.1) to end.
Rounds 11 to 18: As 9 to 2 in reverse.

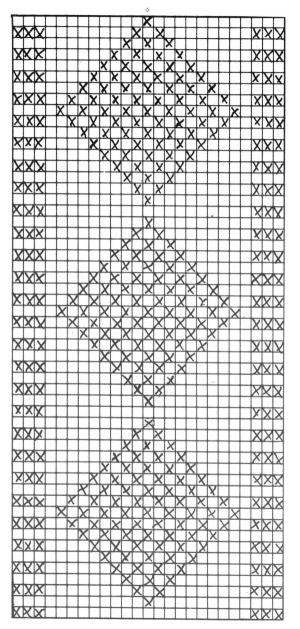

20 Polperro: Snake Cable

24 rounds

Round 1: K.
Round 2: P.2, K.10, P.2, K.8. Repeat to end.
Round 3: K.
Round 4: As 2nd.
Round 5: K.
Round 6: As 2nd.
Round 7: *K.2, P.10, K.2; cable 8 by slipping the first 4 sts. on to cable needle and leaving at **back** of work. Knit the next 4 sts., then the 4 sts. from the spare needle. Repeat from * to end.
Round 8: As 2nd.

Repeat rounds 1 and 2 five times.
Round 19: *K.2, P.10, K.2; cable 8 by slipping the first 4 sts. on to cable needle and leaving at **front** of work. Knit the next 4 sts., then the 4 sts. from the spare needle. Repeat from * to end.
Round 20: As 2nd.

Repeat rounds 1 and 2 twice (24 rounds in all).

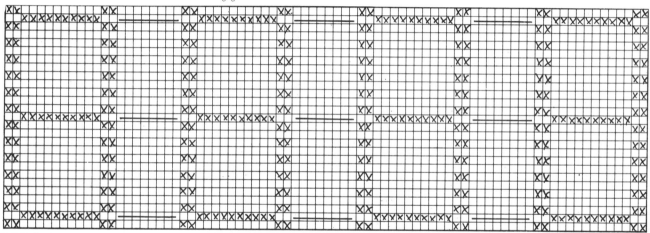

21 Polperro: Horizontal Diamonds

24 rounds

Round 1: K.
Round 2: P.
4 rounds st.-st.
Round 7: K.5; (P.1, K.11) to end.
Round 8: K.4, P.1; (K.1, P.1, K.9, P.1) to end.
Round 9: K.3, P.1, K.1; (K.2, P.1, K.7, P.1, K.1) to end.
Round 10: K.2, P.1, K.2; (K.3, P.1, K.5, P.1, K.2) to end.
Round 11: K.1, P.1, K.3; (K.4, P.1, K.3, P.1, K.3) to end.
Round 12: P.1, K.4; (K.5, P.1, K.1, P.1, K.4) to end.
Round 13: K.5; (K.6, P.1, K.5) to end.

Rounds 14-19: As rounds 12-7 in reverse.
4 rounds st.-st.
Round 24: P.
The bands of pattern are separated by 12 rounds of st.-st., or as required.

*   OR   *

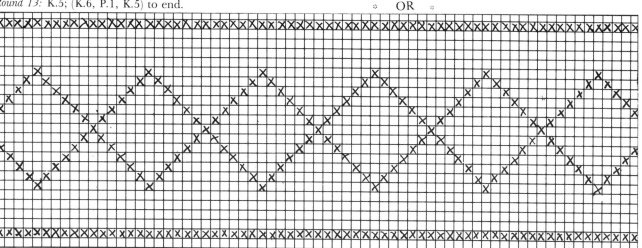

51

Border Patterns

22 Background: Garters or Bars

In circular knitting, work 1 round plain and 1 round purl alternately.

Note: The horizontal lines may be knitted closely together to form a solid pattern area, or separately to divide other pattern areas.

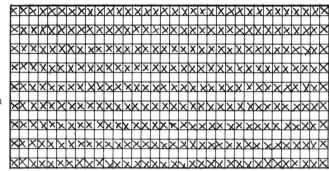

23 Background: Seeding (1)

4-round repeat

Rounds 1 and 3: K.
Round 2: K.2, P.2 to end of round.
Round 4: P.2, K.2 to end of round.

Note: Seeding patterns are commonly used in guernseys,

(a) as horizontal bands; (b) in vertical panels to separate pattern areas; (c) on shoulders, and (d) on sleeve bands.

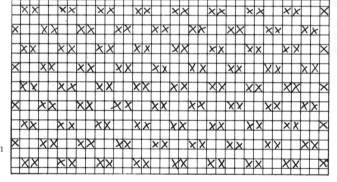

24 Background: Seeding (2)

8-round repeat

Round 1: K.2, P.2 to end.
Round 2 and alternate rounds: K.
Round 3: P.1, (K.2, P.2) to end.
Round 5: P.2, (K.2, P.2) to end.
Round 7: K.1, P.2, (K.2, P.2) to end.

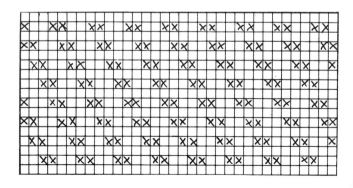

25 Background: Seeding (3) – Moss

4-round repeat

Round 1: K.1, P.1 to end.
Round 2 and alternate rounds: K
Round 3: P.1, K.1 to end.

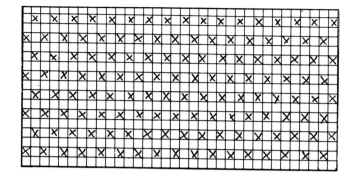

26 Background: Double Moss (Cawsand)

8-round repeat

Round 1 and alternate rounds: K.
Rounds 2 and 4: K.2, P.2 to end
Rounds 6 and 8: P.2, K.2 to end

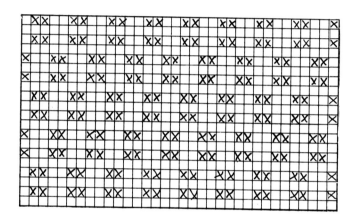

27 Rib 1: 4 plain, 2 garter (Polperro)

Alternate rounds: K.
Alternate rounds: (K.4, P.2) to end.

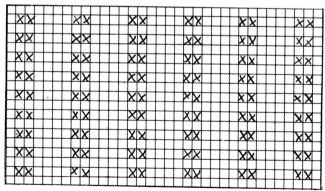

28 Rib 2: Fisherman's Rib (St. Martin's-by-Looe)

This rib is worked over an even number of stitches:

Round 1: (K.1B., P.1) to end.
Round 2: (K.1, P.1B.) to end.

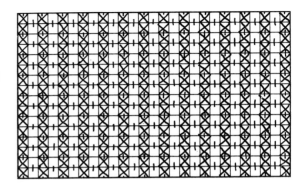

29 Rib 3: 3 plain, 3 garter (St. Ives)

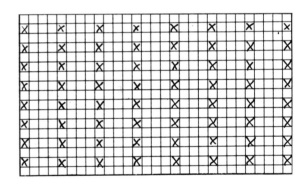

30 Rib 4: 2 plain, 2 garter (Cawsand)

Also known as **Scotch Rib**.

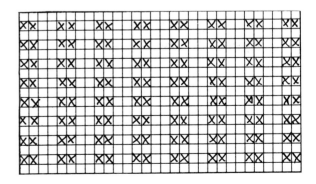

Search On

The Cornish are famous knitsters.

M.A. COURTNEY, Cornish Folk-Lore

In parts of Cornwall where photographic records are not available, the most reliable source of knitting patterns has been personal memory.

Knitters of 150 or 100 years ago had no patterns in written form. They were passed on by word of mouth, and by practical demonstration, from mother to daughter, within families and village communities and sometimes by travellers. People whose memories span sixty years or more can recreate patterns that they frequently saw or heard in their youth. They are able to copy a pattern 'on sight' in knitting or in crochet which they could not translate from written instructions.

From St. Ives, Mrs. Betty Ralph prepared four knitting samples of patterns which she remembered being worked on guernseys fifty or sixty years ago. One is of moss stitch, one of rib, one of an unusual stocking stitch cable and one of a slip stitch pattern.

At Millbrook, Miss Bartlett laid a 1970 guernsey flat on the table and from her memory of the Cawsand guernsey demonstrated how far, how deep and where the patterns of seeding, garters and double moss were positioned.

Mr. Charles Nicholas of Looe remembered his grandmother knitting the 'Eddystone pattern' – recalled by name, but not by knitting detail. However, Mrs. Trathen, also of Looe, remembered women reciting the pattern as they knitted, '7 garters, 5 garters, 3 garters, 1 garter AND 1 garter'. This, translated into plain and purl stitches, produced little lighthouse shapes which gave an interesting texture to the dark navy surface.

A 'double cable' was remembered by two people at Port Isaac. Further investigation revealed that two cables were knitted side by side, the double panel on each side being separated by seeding.

A guernsey 'almost falling to bits' was produced as proof of an Isles of Scilly design. In spite of the rags and tatters, the 'rope' panels were evidently separated by a pattern of garter and slipped stitches. The seeding pattern was also familiar on the Scillies, as a yoke design and on sleeve bands.

A total of ten individual patterns have been recorded from Polperro. 'Seeds and bars' was the most common and the best remembered: 'Most of Mr. Broad's

ABOVE *Charles 'Fay' Jolliff wearing the 'seeds and bars' pattern at Polperro in the 1950s.*

RIGHT *The same pattern was recorded at Whitby, Yorkshire, in the 1850s. This photograph, taken by Frank Meadow Sutcliffe, is of Henry Freeman, lifeboatman and sole survivor of the Whitby lifeboat disaster of 1861 when 12 men were drowned.*

knitters did the "seeds and bars".' It is a simple and effective design, recorded photographically in 1850 and in 1950 in both Cornwall and Whitby. It is particularly common in sleeve bands. The seeding effect is achieved by alternating groups of purl stitches: i.e., 1 plain, 1 purl on one row; 1 purl, 1 plain on another *or* 2 plain, 2 purl on one row; 2 purl, 2 plain on another, *but* with a plain row always separating the patterned rows. In this way, the purl stitches (seeds) stand out prominently.

It is interesting to record the clever balance of pattern area, which was instinctively created by experienced knitters. One 'seeding' pattern was worked over four rows. 'Bars' were single garter stitch lines worked every four rows. A pattern area with 4 bars (16 rows) was balanced by 4 repeats of seeding (16 rows); with 3 bars, 12 rows of seeding (3 repeats) are visible. For variations in size, the number of stocking stitch rows between bars and adjoining seed bands was increased, but the balanced weight of design remained the same.

Some cables were used, with one almost identical to Mr. Stephens' pattern from the Lizard. One lady said that her mother did 'seeds between cables, but did not use a third needle for the cable'. The most distinctive pattern so far recorded is the 'snake' cable.

'Everyday' knit-frocks were usually patterned in rib, with '4 plain, 2 garter' being the most common. There were no problems of identification, even with several men and boys in one family. The knitter used her own initiative in variations of the depths of the ribbed yoke, a broken line, the rib width or the sleeve detail. Initials were sometimes knitted in an area of stocking stitch and occasionally the name of the boat was included. The Reverend Robert Stephen Hawker had a small red cross woven into one side of his guernsey as a symbol of the 'centurion's cruel spear'. In this way a guernsey became a very personal gift from maker to wearer.

An unusual sleeve band on a ribbed knit-frock from Polperro.

In The Round

The construction of a guernsey in the traditional way is a specialised technique. Using the correct yarn and a set of long stocking needles, stitches are cast on and worked 'in the round' to armhole level. A single garter stitch marks each side and acts as a guide for shaping; and an underarm gusset, made by increasing and decreasing from the seam stitches, links the body to the sleeve.

Front and back yokes are worked separately, on two needles, and the two sets of shoulder stitches are joined, either by grafting or by knitting a seam.

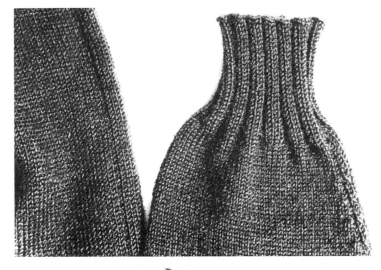

Lines formed by seam stitches as seen on sides and sleeves.

The upper half of a guernsey showing pattern and underarm gusset.

The neckband is knitted according to the preference of the wearer. Some like a band fitted close to the neck, some like a higher neckline which turns over, and some prefer a loose style, one or two inches (2.5 - 5 cm) away from the neck. The latter is made possible by triangular gussets knitted at the neck end of each shoulder line *before* the stitches are picked up around the neck. (For details, *see* pattern for a Polperro knit-frock, pp.66-7).

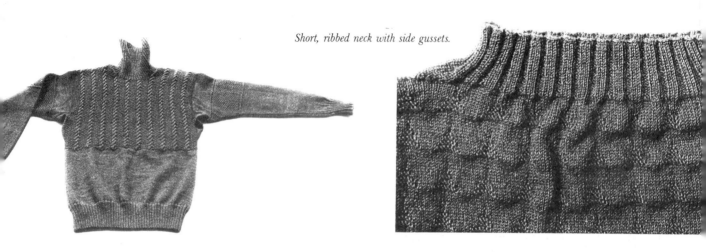

Short, ribbed neck with side gussets.

Guernsey with high neck. The yoke design was copied from William Stephens' photograph.

Sleeve stitches are picked up around the armhole with the underarm gusset stitches, and knitted downwards 'in the round', decreasing as required and casting off at the cuff, thus completing the seamless garment. The elbow and cuff areas frequently take the hardest wear, and renewal is quite simple: the sleeve is unravelled from the cuff as far as necessary, and re-knitted.

SPLICING is the best method of joining wool in circular knitting and is an adaptation of the seafarer's method of splicing rope.

Method
1. Unravel the strands at the ends of old and new yarn (about 2.5 cm [1 inch] per ply, *i.e.* 10 cm [4 inches] for a four-ply yarn);
2. Layer the strands equally by trimming, 1, 2, 3, 4 : 4, 3, 2, 1;
3. Place opposite strands so that they overlap slightly;
4. Dampen the fingers and roll strands firmly together;
5. Twist spliced length carefully and thoroughly when knitting.

In Cornish guernseys, the base line is knitted in rib, sometimes with the yarn used double for extra strength. The thumb method of casting on gives greatest elasticity and is the most suitable for circular knitting.

The patterned area of guernseys is concentrated in the upper half of the garment. Rib patterns are sometimes used; alternatively, combinations of vertical panels or horizontal bands make a wider pattern right across the front and back. A narrow band of pattern is commonly introduced as a border and echoed on the shoulder or upper sleeve.

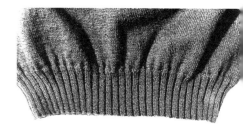

Deep, firm rib at welt, as seen in most Cornish guernseys.

BELOW: *A 1972 interpretation of the knit-frock worn by Jim Curtis in the photograph, below left.*

Charles Jolliffe, Charles Jolliffe, Jnr., and Jim Curtis with a young friend at Polperro in the 1860s. Note the knitted braces.

In the Channel Islands, the construction varies in the base line and armhole edge. The base line is formed by a specialised knotted edge,* worked separately for front and back, and joined in a circle after about twenty-four rows. Traditionally, the body fabric is worked in the round *to shoulder level*. Knitted stitches are then cut to form the armhole, and the sleeves are knitted from the cuff and sewn into the armhole.

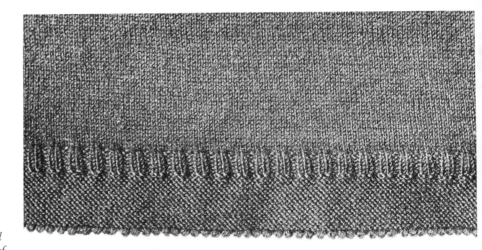

Knotted edge, garter border and margin rib – all characteristic of traditional Channel Islands guernseys.

---

* To make the Channel Islands knotted edge, fold in half about 2 metres of wool, to be used double, in the left hand, throughout the cast-on line. Stitches are knitted onto the right-hand needle with single wool, and the first loop will be made at the meeting point of double and single strands. Then (wind wool twice anticlockwise around the thumb, knit stitch through all 4 strands; bring wool forward and around needle as for 'make 1') thereby making two stitches each time. Repeat from () to end. Continuing with a single strand from the main ball of wool, knit back one row, thus forming the knots. Knit several rows of garter stitch to follow.

Cornish Guernsey, Basic Pattern

These instructions are for a guernsey in plain knitted fabric, *i.e.* stocking stitch. Any pattern or combination of patterns shown in chart or written form in this book (pp. 31-54) may be inserted at appropriate stages.

Allow extra wool when cable patterns are used.

Important
When choosing a pattern, remember that the centre point of each pattern chart (marked* if applicable) must be centred on the knitting. A coloured marker on the central stitch of front and back is a good guide. Panels or margins of seeding or background pattern may be used to balance the number of stitches. (See pattern of Polperro knit-frock, pp.66-7, for ideas.)

Materials

5 *ply worsted yarn*, obtainable from Poppleton's agencies* in Cornwall and the Channel Islands:

8 × 100g
9 × 100g

Needles, size 2¼ mm (13): 1 circular, 1 set of four, and 1 long pair.

Tension
18 sts. and 20 rows to 5 cm (2 ins.).

Measurements
Chest sizes: 92-102 cm (36-40 ins.);
102-112 cm (40-44 ins.).
Length from shoulder, 69 cm (27 ins.).
Sleeve seam, 48 cm (19 ins.).

Note: TEST TENSION FIRST

---

* Poppleton's 5-ply guernsey wool is available to personal and postal shoppers from The Wool Shop, 6 Pike Street, Liskeard, Cornwall PL14 3JE (tel. Liskeard 42375), and The Wool Basket, 38 Fore Street, Redruth, Cornwall TR15 2AE (tel. Redruth 215634). It is sometimes available from other shops in Cornwall.

METHOD

Using the circular needle, cast on 336 sts. (372 sts.). Check that the sts. are not twisted before joining into a round. Work in K.3, P.3 rib for 8 cm (3 ins.), O.R.L., increasing 12 sts. evenly on the last round. 348 sts. (384 sts.).

* Mark the middle stitch of the last P.3. with a double marker for the first seam st. and the middle stitch of a P.3 on the opposite side with a single marker for the second seam st. These single sts. will continue up each side as garter sts. (one round a plain st., one round a purl st.), and will be referred to as 'seam sts.'*

From the rib, continue in st.-st. until work measures 36 cm (14 ins.), O.R.L.

* At this point, pattern and gussets begin. The gussets are worked in st.-st. and are made by increasing from the seam-st. on every 4th. row (2 sts. on each gusset every 4 rows). The first inc. will be from the seam-st., thus: inc. on EACH side of seam-st. (3 from 1). The two inc. sts. will now become seam-sts. on each side of the gusset, and the middle st. forms the apex of the gusset.

Underarm gusset, shaped by increasing from the seam stitch. The stitches are left on a holder until required for knitting the sleeve.

Continue until work measures 46 cm (18 ins.) at armhole level. There will now be 25 sts. for each underarm gusset and 173 (191) sts. for front and back. Transfer the gusset sts. to holders while knitting continues in two equal sections, front and back, on TWO needles. Care should be taken to adjust reading of patterns and charts accordingly.

Five sts. at each end of needle are worked as garter-st., to form a shoulder 'strap'.
The first two rows on the front will read thus:
1. K.5, pattern to last 5 sts., K.5.
2. K.5, pattern (reverse side) to last 5 sts., K.5.

Continue until armhole measures 20 cm (8 ins.). Divide sts. so that 58 (64) are used for each shoulder and 57 (63) are placed on holder for neck.

SHOULDER

Work 12 rows in garter-st. or one of the border patterns, decreasing one st. at neck edge on 3rd. and 7th. rows. Leave these sts. on a holder or the knitting needle.

Complete back to match front. Join one pair of shoulder sts. together by (a) grafting, or (b) knitting off. The latter process is worked by placing the two sets of sts. together, wrong sides facing, and, with a third needle, casting off. One stitch from the front needle and one stitch from the back needle are knitted together AS ONE during the casting-off. Work the second shoulder likewise.

NECK

Pick up and knit 162 (174) sts. around neck (57 [63] from each holder and 24 from each shoulder edge). Work in K.3, P.3 rib for 15 rounds or depth required.

SLEEVES

Pick up and knit 132 sts. around armhole, plus 2 seam sts., plus 25 gusset sts. The gusset sts. are worked in st.-st., decreasing 1 st. each side, every 4th. round until single seam-st. remains. If desired, a pattern band may be worked on the main sleeve area, directly from the armhole edge or after a margin of st.-st.

On completion of gusset, continue sleeve in st.-st., keeping seam-st. in garter-st. as before. Dec. each side of it every 4th. round 10 times, then every 5th. round until 79 sts. remain. Knit the last 2 sts. together (78 sts.). Continue in st. st. until sleeve measures 39 cm (15½ ins.), O.R.L.

Finish with cuff in K.3, P.3 rib for 8 cm (3 ins.). Cast off in rib.
Work the second sleeve likewise.

Pattern for a Polperro Knit-Frock

This design is based on the knit-frock worn by one of the musicians in the group of village lads, shown in one of the photographs taken by Lewis Harding in the mid-nineteenth century. The pattern is worked in 4-ply worsted, on needles size 2¾ mm (12) or 2¼ mm (13), and incorporates a neck gusset.

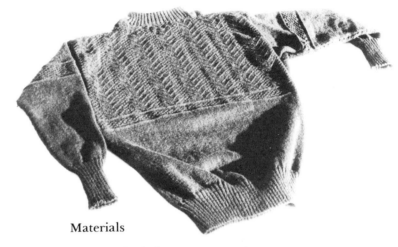

A Polperro knit-frock copied from the 'Boy Musicians' photograph on page 16.

Materials

6(7) × 100g 4 ply guernsey wool.

Needles: 1 circular 76 cm (30″), 1 pair long and 6 stocking needles, all in size 2¼ mm (13) for the smaller size and size 2¾ mm (12) for the larger size.

Tension

18 (16) sts. to 5 cm (2 ins.),
22 (20) rows to 5 cm (2 ins.).

Measurements

Chest sizes: 92-97 cm (36-38 ins.)
102-107 cm (40-42 ins.)
Length from shoulder: 64 (67) cm (25 [26½] ins.)
Sleeve seam: 48 (53) cm (19 [21] ins.)

Note: Where appropriate, instructions for the larger size will be in brackets ( )

METHOD

Using the circular needle appropriate to size, cast on 340 sts. in the round and work in K.2, P.2 rib for 8 cm (3 ins.) or 9 cm (3½ ins.). Cont. in st.-st., marking one st. each side as a seam st. (to be worked one round in plain, one round in purl) until work measures 30 (34) cm, (12 [13½] ins.).

Now commence border pattern and gusset shaping.

Next round: (P. to first seam st., inc. ONE st. each side of seam st.). Repeat once.

Continue working border pattern with 4 rounds st.-st., 7 rounds seeding, 4 rounds st-st., 1 round garter. AT THE SAME TIME, work gussets on each side by using the two first increases as seam sts. and the sts. between in st.-st. Inc. 2 sts. every 4th round until there are 27 sts. altogether.

Begin MAIN pattern (see p.47) after border pattern has been completed. When gussets have been worked, leave sts. on a holder, and cont. front and back yokes separately on two long needles, until work measures 64 (67) cm, (25 [26½] ins.).

Note: Care must be taken to adapt chart and instructions to 2-way knitting.

SHOULDER

Place the two sets of sts. together and, *working from the shoulder edge, cast off 50 sts. from each needle, knitting a stitch from front and back AS ONE.

With 1 st. left on the cast-off needle, the neck gusset begins:

K.1 from front needle. Turn and slip the first st. purlwise. P. the next st. and 1 from back needle. Turn and cont. taking 1 more st. alternately from front and back until there are 21 sts. on needle.* This completes the first gusset. Leave these sts. on a holder.

Work other side to match, from * to *.

NECK

Work 14 rounds in K.2, P.2 rib on sts. assembled from the two neck gussets, the front and back. Cast off in rib.

SLEEVES

Using stocking needles, pick up and knit 130 sts. around armhole plus gusset sts. plus seam sts. The sleeve is worked in st.-st. for 10 cm (4 ins.) with a band of 'seeding' (1 round garter, 4 rounds st.-st., 19 rounds 'seeding', 4 rounds st.-st., 1 round garter), then st.-st. to rib level.

Decreasings are worked *within* seam sts. until gusset is completed, then *each side* of seam sts. Decrease 2 sts. every 4th round until there are 73 sts., and cont. in st.-st. until work measures 39 cm (15½ ins), (44 cm [17½ ins.]), decreasing 1 st. on the last round (72 sts.).

Work in K.2, P.2 rib for 9 cm (3½ ins.). Cast off in rib.

Bibliography

Allen, John, *A History of Liskeard,* Cash, London, 1856.

de Burlet, Sheila, *Portrait of Polperro,* Rooster, Falmouth, 1977.

Byles, *Life and Letters of Robert Stephen Hawker,* John Lane, Bodley Head, London, 1905.

Couch, Johathan, *History of Polperro,* 1871 (manuscript).

Courtney, M.A., *Cornish Feasts and Folk-Lore,* Beare, Penzance, 1890, and E.P. Publishing, 1973.

Gay, Susan E., *Old Falmouth,* Headley, London, 1903.

Harlow, Eve, (*ed.*), *The Art of Knitting,* Collins, Glasgow and London, 1977.

Hartley, M., and Ingilby, J., *The Old Hand-Knitters of the Dales,* Dalesman Press, Yorkshire, 1951 and 1969.

Jenkin, A.K. Hamilton, *The Cornish Miner,* David and Charles, 1972 (also 1927, 1948, 1962).

Jenkin, A.K. Hamilton, *Cornwall and its People*, Dent, London, 1945, and David and Charles, Newton Abbot, 1970.
(This is an omnibus edition of *Cornish Seafarers,* 1932, *Cornwall and the Cornish,* 1933, and *Cornish Homes and Customs,* 1934, all published by Dent.)

Jersey Island Federation of Womens Institutes, *Jerseys Old and New,* 1978.

Kelly's *Directories of Cornwall,* 1873-1935.

Lanyon, Andrew, *The Rooks of Trelawne,* Photographer's Gallery, London, 1976.

Paynter, S. Winifred, *Old St. Ives.*

Thompson, Gladys, *Patterns for Guernseys and Jerseys,* Batsford, London, 1969 (revised edition of *Guernsey and Jersey Patterns,* 1955). Another edition, *Patterns for Guernseys, Jerseys and Arans,* Dover, New York, 1971, revised ed. 1974.

Thomas, Mary, *Mary Thomas's Knitting Book,* Hodder and Stoughton, London, 1938 (Dover, New York, 1972).

Veall, Martin, and Harris, James Howard, *Porthleven Past and Present,* 1885.

Cornish Times newspapers

West Briton newspapers

Official Census Returns, 1841, 1851, 1861, 1901.